MW01131895

Visit our website to take the Growth Mindset Course.

www.kidyouniversity.com

Who is this for?

This journal was made for **YOU.**
The world is a better place because you are in it.

You are magic!

Let's talk about

about

GROWTH MINDSET

A ten-day challenge journal for kids

GAHMYA DRUMMOND-BEY

What is a challenge journal?

What is a challenge?

When someone invites you to participate in a challenge, it is a way for you to learn and grow. A challenge usually lasts for a certain number of days.

What is a challenge journal?

A challenge journal teaches you lessons while you take your challenge. You will have a place to write and draw your ideas as you learn new things.

What is my mission for this challenge journal?

Your mission for this journal is to learn what it means to have a growth mindset and to start thinking with a growth mindset.

What is a growth mindset?

People who have a growth mindset think positively and know that they can always get better, learn, and grow. Thinking with a growth mindset will help you to have more confidence and feel excited to try even more new things.

How does the challenge journal work?

 ## Choose your challenge style

There are different ways to take your challenge.
You can take the challenge with this book.
(That's all you need!)
You could also take the challenge with the book and the animated challenge course on www.kidyouniversity.com.

 ## Choose your start day

This is a ten-day challenge! It has two parts and each part runs for five days.
It works best if you can do the challenge every day for ten days. Choose the day you want to start.

 ## Choose your Challenge Friend

It helps to have a friend to do your challenge with. You can do the challenge alone, but there are days when it will be useful to have a partner.

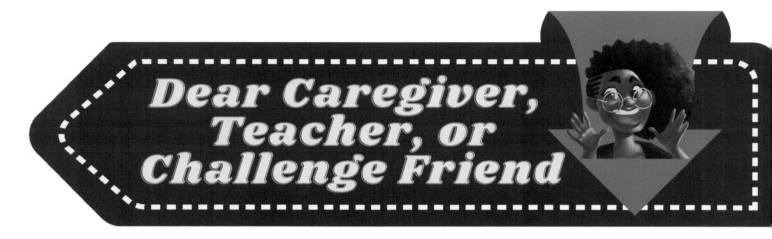

Dear Caregiver, Teacher, or Challenge Friend

What an incredible journey!

Ask Me About Growth Mindset gives you the opportunity to not only open up a new world of possibility and courage for the child you are supporting with this journal, but it is also a great bonding experience for the two of you.

Be as present as you can.
Share your own personal stories.
Add "challenge time" to your daily schedule for the next ten days.
Show excitement! The energy that you bring to the space is most important.

So many of us grow up thinking that personal growth and even therapy are ways to fix parts of ourselves that are broken. However, by engaging in this ten-day challenge, you are modeling that self-improvement is an exciting everyday process.
This is a true gift!

Enjoy!

THIS CHALLENGE IS ACCEPTED BY:

My name is

_____

My Challenge Friend is

_____

After the challenge, we will celebrate by

_____

CHALLENGE CHECK LIST

This is your challenge checklist.
The challenge will last for ten days.
After you complete each day, color in the box for
that day. This will help you to stay on track.

DAY 1

DAY 2

DAY 3

DAY 4

DAY 5

DAY 1

DAY 2

DAY 3

DAY 4

DAY 5

What is a Growth Mindset?

"Mindset" means the way you think.

Some people have a GROWTH MINDSET. Someone with a growth mindset has a positive mindset and usually looks for good things to happen. When someone has a growth mindset, they focus on their effort because they know that they can do anything as long as they keep trying and learning.

People with growth mindsets know that we can always get better, mistakes help us grow, and every day is a new day to try again!

Having a Growth Mindset is GREAT! In this challenge, we will learn more about having a growth mindset. We will also practice thinking with a growth mindset because anyone can learn to have a growth mindset.

You can choose your

Mindset

PART 1

We can always get better, mistakes help us grow, and every day is a new day to try again! Are you ready to learn a super skill? Let's go! You're going to need your Challenge friend (or someone else you trust) for the next page.

> You and your Challenge Friend both have BIG DREAMS!
>
> Having a Growth Mindset helps us to make our big dreams come true!

What is one way you would make the world a better place?

ME

MY FRIEND

What is one way you would make the world a better place?

- Draw your answers. Then, explain them to each other.

- Choose a bracelet from the next page!

MANTRA BRACELETS

These are your special bracelets.
Cut out each strip. Wear the bracelet that you choose today.
Share them with friends!

NO EXCUSES!

I BELIEVE IN MYSELF

I HAVE BIG GOALS

I WILL TRY A NEW THING

TODAY, I WILL TRY.

I AM A UNICORN

I GET BETTER EVERYDAY

I AM LOVED

I LOVE MYSELF

MISTAKES HELP ME GROW

I AM A GOOD FRIEND

I AM HELPFUL

I LOVE CHALLENGES!

TODAY, I AM BRAVE

MEET MISTY DAY 1

You can learn and grow

Misty Copeland is a famous ballet dancer.
But, it was not easy for her to become a famous ballerina.

Many ballet dancers begin to learn ballet when they are very young, but Misty Copeland started to learn ballet when she was 13.
People with a fixed mindset may think, "13 is too old to learn ballet, she can never make it."
But, Misty Copeland had a growth mindset and thought,

"I can learn and try my best!"

Misty Copeland did not have a lot of money. She had 6 siblings to share things with. If Misty had a fixed mindset, she may have thought, "I can't learn ballet because it is only for rich people."

But, Misty Copeland had a growth mindset.
So, what do you think she told herself, instead?

I think she told herself something like,
"Anyone can learn ballet and I'm going to
find a way!"

Misty Copeland danced and danced! She even danced for the American Ballet Theatre, which is an AMAZING place for dancers!

But, Misty Copeland experienced some racism there. Racism involves thinking with a fixed mindset.

It's when people think that one group of people, who look a certain way, is better than another group, who look different than the first group. But, we are not all meant to look the same, right?

When Misty danced, there were not many other Black ballet dancers like her.

Some of the other ballerinas had a fixed mindset and said racist things to Misty like, "tutus don't look good on Black women." Of course, that is not true, but I'm sure that made Misty sad.

Misty did not give up. She knew that Black women and girls could be great ballerinas. Boys can be great ballet dancers! You could be a great ballet dancer, too!

Misty kept dancing and she made history!
She became the first Black ballet dancer to be a principal dancer at the American Ballet Theatre.
That means that she became a top dancer in the whole ballet company! Wow!

THINK ABOUT IT

Do you remember a time when you tried your best? What were you doing?

_____

_____

Misty's Mirror

Imagine if Misty could see the messages you wrote on her mirror right now! Could you write some messages on her mirror to encourage her to keep going?

DAY 1 CHALLENGE

Today's challenge is to give 7 compliments!

Your voice is powerful and the words you say can really help others to have a growth mindset and feel good about themselves. Give 7 compliments to anyone you want today.
(It doesn't have to be the same person each time.)
Let's use the power of your voice for good!

Compliment Tracker

Color one microphone after you give a compliment. When you have colored all 7, you are done!

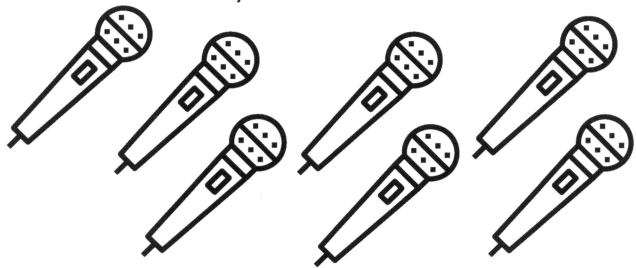

MEET MICHAEL JORDAN

Michael Jordan is a famous athlete. Many people believe that he is the greatest basketball player in the world! Some people called him "Air Jordan" because of how high he could jump and dunk a basketball.

He is also the first basketball player to be a billionaire.

Keep Practicing!

Michael Jordan loved sports! When he was a high school student, he didn't make the basketball team. If he had a fixed mindset, he may have thought,

"I'm just not good at basketball, I should give up!"

But, he had a growth mindset, so he did not give up. He made the basketball team the next year! Wow!

Michael kept practicing and he kept getting better!

He even went to college and played basketball there! Michael played basketball at the University of North Carolina. In college, he became the basketball player of the year! Wow! Then, he went to play in the NBA. He played basketball in front of lots and lots of people.

He even played basketball on television! Soon, Michael played championship basketball games. When a basketball team wins a championship, all of the players on that team win a championship ring.

Michael Jordan won 6 championships with his basketball team, the Chicago Bulls. So, he won 6 championship rings!

Michael Jordan became a famous basketball player!
He even traveled the world to play in the Olympics.
But, guess what? He made lots of mistakes and sometimes he
lost games and his ball didn't make it in the hoop!

But, Michael Jordan said that it's okay to fail and make
mistakes. But, to him, it's not okay if you don't try.

It's very important to try.

What do you think about that?
I think that he had a great growth mindset! When we have a
growth mindset, we know that mistakes help us get better.

We also know that sometimes when people win a lot, they also
lose a lot. It's okay not to win every single time.

It's also okay to make mistakes! Yes!!

THINK ABOUT IT

Do you remember a time when you tried something
and failed? What did you learn from that?

_____

_____

_____

DAY 2 CHALLENGE

Your challenge
today is to think of something that is
tough for you and make a poster that
reminds you to keep going.
You can make your poster here:

RONNIE'S POWER OF YET!

Ronnie has been trying and trying, but he just can't make a jump shot.

It's just so far!

Ronnie went to the playground to watch the big guys play.

It's all about balance!

Then, he went back home to try to copy them!

Maybe I should just try another sport.

Ronnie began to doubt himself.

Meet Your Mindset

Let's look at what it's like to think with a fixed mindset and what it's like to think with a growth mindset.

CHOOSE YOUR MINDSET

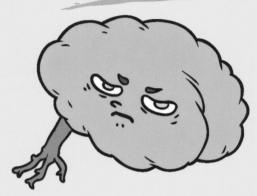

When someone is thinking with a fixed mindset, they may say, **"If I get a bad grade, that means I'm just not good at it."**

But, a person with a growth mindset may say, **"If I get a bad grade, I can learn from my mistakes and do better next time."**

When someone is thinking with a fixed mindset, they may say, **"I don't like to see others doing better than me."**

With a GROWTH MINDSET, that person could think, **"I love when others do well too! We can all do great things!"**

Thinking with a fixed mindset could sound like, **"If something is too hard, I just give up."**

But, if we flip that into a growth mindset, we could think, **"I love challenges!"**

Kemi's hair worry

Kemi does not like her hair today.
Yesterday, she loved her afro.
But, she wants another hairstyle today.
"My hair is bad!" Kemi says to her Mom.
"Kemi, my love, you have beautiful hair.
Your hair is not bad!" her mom said.

Kemi's hair love

Help Kemi to love her hair and use a growth mindset.
Color each Crown that has a growth mindset phrase.

"Let's try a different hairstyle!"

"Let's watch a YOUTUBE video for hair tips."

"Hair like yours cannot grow."

"That's okay. I don't like my hair either."

"Hair can do so many things! Don't give up!"

"Don't you wish you had hair like mine?"

Your hair is beautiful and so are you!

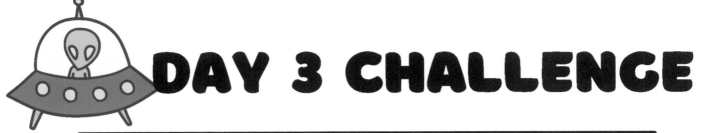

DAY 3 CHALLENGE

Your challenge today is to think about 3 parts of yourself (for example: my hair, my eyes, my legs). Draw a picture of each in the cloud. Then, write a thank you note to that part of yourself and why you love it.

Thank you to my _____

because _____

_____

Thank you to my _____

because _____

_____

Thank you to my _____

because _____

_____

COOL AND SPECIAL ME

You are cool and special just the way you are.
Draw yourself here. Draw your favorite clothes, your
favorite hairstyle. Draw yourself looking the way you
love to look.

BONUS CHALLENGE

Try to wear your
favorite thing
or style tomorrow.

Today's Challenge:
Thank different parts of yourself
and wear your favorite style

Mistakes Are for Learning

Everyone makes mistakes.
Sometimes, we become
embarrassed after we make a
mistake. Then, we are afraid to try
something new again.
But, that's a fixed mindset.

When we have a growth mindset,
we know that every mistake helps
us learn something new.
Mistakes help us grow!

THINK ABOUT IT

**Tell me about a time you made a
mistake. What happened?**

_____

_____

_____

LIL MAMA'S BIG MISTAKE

Lil Mama is a rapper and an actress.
One time, she made a big mistake.
While at a concert, Lil Mama was really excited to hear her favorite song. So, she jumped on stage during the performance. But, many people were not happy about that. It is not nice to jump on a stage when someone is performing unless you are invited.

Lil Mama was very embarrassed.

But, that mistake taught her a big lesson about kindness and being patient. After that mistake, Lil Mama made more of her own songs! Mistakes help us grow!

DAY 4 CHALLENGE

Your challenge today is to think about some of your mistakes. Write your mistakes inside the circle. Then, cut out the circle. Crumple the circle into a ball in your hand. Holding the ball, close your eyes, and thank your mistakes for helping you grow. Then, throw the ball in the trash.

GROWTH MINDSET WITH ALLAHNA AND RONNIE

Allahna loves to try to spell new words!

I love to grow my brain!

Ronnie loves to spell new words, too. But spelling tests make him nervous.

I'm just not good at spelling!

Last week, Allahna asked her friend, Tayo, for help!

That's what friends are for!

Every time you TRY, your brain gets stronger!

Ronnie didn't want help from Tayo.

I'll never spell as well as Tayo!

When Allahna makes mistakes, she practices again!

Sometimes, Ronnie hides his mistakes.

He doesn't want anyone to see them.

Allahna's mom likes when Allahna tries!

That's right! Just try your best!

Sometimes Ronnie is afraid to try. He doesn't want to mess up.

Allahna has a growth mindset. She knows that she can grow her brain. She also loves to learn from her mistakes!

That's right! I'm teaching Ronnie to have a growth mindset, too!

Thanks Allahna! I am going to practce spelling with you! I want to grow my brain!

Learn From Others

When someone has a growth mindset, they understand that people aren't just born smart. When you make an effort and keep trying, you can get better at things. Making an effort means giving something all you've got.

Sometimes, that means learning from others.

We can learn so much from others, especially when we pay attention and listen carefully.

Stories are a great way to learn, too!
You can learn a lot from reading books and from listening to people's stories.

THINK ABOUT IT

What's your favorite story?

DAY 5 CHALLENGE

It's storytelling time!

Find a Challenge Friend. Your Challenge Friend can be a family member, a friend, or the person you chose at the beginning of this journal. Choose someone who is older than you.

Ask them this question:

"Can you tell me a story about your favorite mistake? What did you learn?"

My challenge friend's name is

Right now, I feel

Today's Challenge:
Ask a challenge friend about their favorite mistake. Listen to their story.

You are Special

_____
_____

Be Yourself

_____
_____

PART 2

_____

There's no one in the world exactly like you. You are so special and important just the way you are! Remember to be kind to yourself, love yourself, and even say nice things to yourself.

Treat yourself the way you treat your very best friend.

There is only one YOU

MEET AMANDA GORMAN

Amanda Gorman is an American poet and activist. She was born in California.
She also has a twin sister.
Lots of people became fans of Amanda when she recited her poem, "The Hill We Climb," at President Joe Biden's inauguration.

Amanda made history because she was the youngest poet to ever recite a poem at a president's inauguration in the United States.
But, speaking in public was not always easy for Amanda.

Amanda has a speech impediment. When someone has a speech impediment, that means it may be hard for them to speak clearly or for others to understand what they are saying.

When Amanda was growing up, it was hard for her to say words with the "r" sound.

If Amanda would've had a fixed mindset, she may have thought, "I can never be a poet." But, Amanda has a growth mindset! She knew that she could practice and she did. Amanda used writing and poetry to practice speaking more clearly.

She still has some trouble with pronouncing words with the letter "r" and that's okay! Amanda Gorman is a great poet!

THINK ABOUT IT

Is there something that is challenging for you to do? What is it?

Things I Can Tell Myself

Cut out the phrases below. Then, match the
fixed mindset quote and the growth mindset quote.

Fixed Mindset → Growth Mindset

Fixed Mindset		Growth Mindset
	→	
	→	
	→	
	→	
	→	

I'm a problem solver!	I don't want to try!
I can do hard things!	I can try another way!
Mistakes help me learn!	I quit!
That never works for me!	I always mess up!
I never give up!	I can't do this!

What's My Mindset And What's Your Advice?

Draw a line to match the way of thinking to the mindset.
Then, match the mindset to the blue advice box that's best.

I fell down today! I won't ever skate again!

I have a spelling test soon. I will practice every day! I will keep getting better!

I am not good at math. My dad is bad at math, too!

GROWTH MINDSET

FIXED MINDSET

FIXED MINDSET

Keep trying! You will get better every day!

Yes! You will keep learning, just like me!

You aren't good at math . . . YET! Keep trying! Your dad can get better too!

DAY 1 CHALLENGE

It's time to spread kindness!

It's great to have a growth mindset.
However, sometimes it can be challenging for us
to have a growth mindset on our difficult days.
Your goal is to add more positivity to the world
by doing 5 kind things.

Color one section on the number 5 until the
entire number has been colored. You've got this!

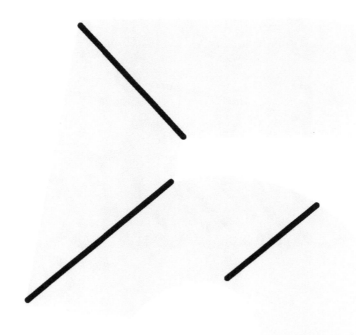

Follow Your Heart
MEET MAURICE ASHLEY

Maurice Ashley is the first Black Grandmaster of Chess in the world!
When someone is a chess "Grandmaster," that means they have reached the highest title that someone can reach as a professional chess player, other than being World Champion.

In order to become a Grandmaster, Maurice Ashley had to believe in himself.

People who become a Grandmaster usually start learning how to play chess and competing against others at a young age.

However, Maurice Ashley didn't really learn how to play chess until he was fourteen years old. He'd moved from Jamaica to the United States. In the United States, he lived in New York City and had a chance to learn to play chess in school.

He really wanted to be great, but his family didn't think he could make much money playing chess and thought he should focus on other things.

But, Maurice had a growth mindset. Sometimes, people around us may not have a growth mindset and we have to believe in ourselves the most.

Maurice Ashley believed in himself and became a Grandmaster! Wow! He made his family proud and he was also very proud of himself!

THINK ABOUT IT

How do you think Maurice Ashley felt when his family didn't support his dream?

_____

What is one thing you wish your family supported you with more?

_____

My "Good Day" Mirror

Write a special note to yourself on the mirror!
Now, practice reading it to yourself! As you read it, feel yourself
becoming fiilled with energy and confidence! You're amazing!

DAY 2 CHALLENGE

Positive Energy Everywhere!

Sometimes we have to be cheerleaders and motivators for ourselves. But, it's also great to cheer others on! Write positive messages on the squares below. Then, cut them out and hide them in places for others to find.

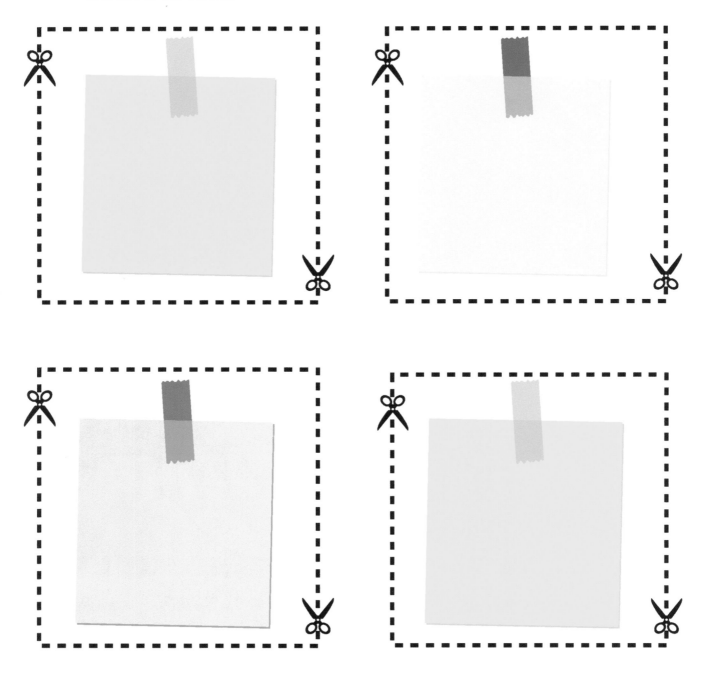

Your Supporters

DAY 3

Who can you go to for support?
When we have a growth mindset, not only can we cheer ourselves on, but we can also ask for help.
No one is perfect. We are all special and that's so beautiful.
Let's think of some of your supporters today. Your supporters are people who encourage you. Write the names of your supporters on the rainbow. Then, color the rainbow.

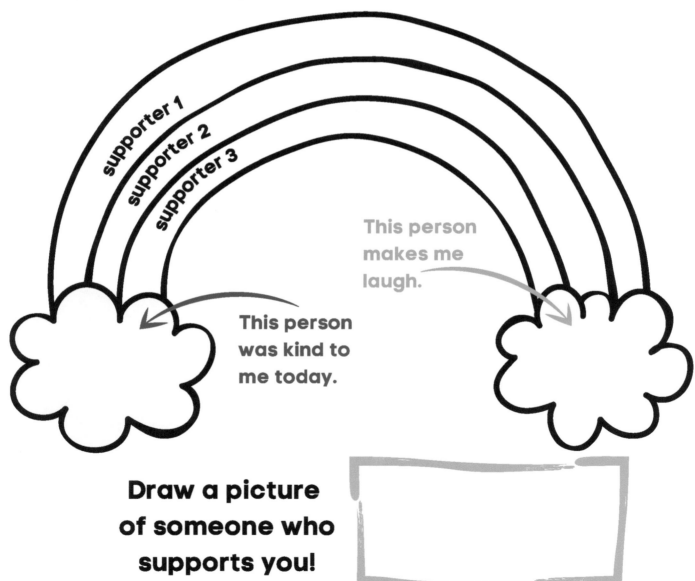

supporter 1
supporter 2
supporter 3

This person makes me laugh.

This person was kind to me today.

Draw a picture of someone who supports you!

Color By Mindset

Do you know the difference between
a growth mindset phrase and a fixed mindset phrase?

Color all of the growth mindset phrases shades of purple.
Color all of the fixed mindset phrases shades of blue.

Key

Growth Mindset

Fixed Mindset

Day 3

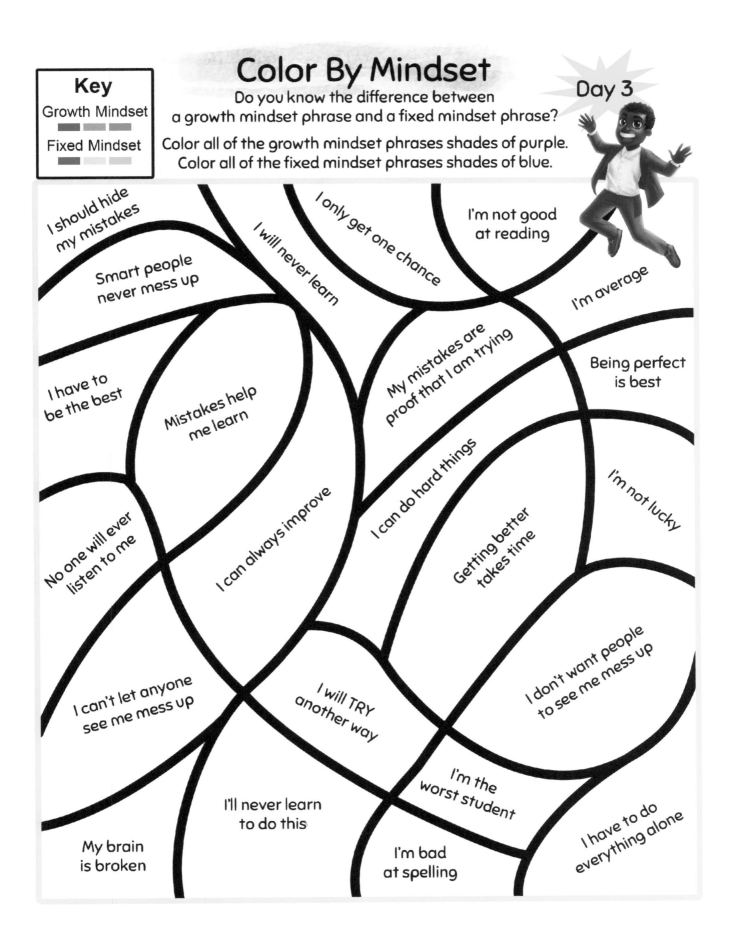

I should hide my mistakes

Smart people never mess up

I will never learn

I only get one chance

I'm not good at reading

I'm average

I have to be the best

Mistakes help me learn

My mistakes are proof that I am trying

Being perfect is best

No one will ever listen to me

I can always improve

I can do hard things

Getting better takes time

I'm not lucky

I can't let anyone see me mess up

I will TRY another way

I don't want people to see me mess up

My brain is broken

I'll never learn to do this

I'm the worst student

I'm bad at spelling

I have to do everything alone

My Try Again Maze

Help Ronnie through the maze.
When you help him through the maze,
he will take the basketball to the hoop!

THANKS FOR HELPING ME!

DAY 3 CHALLENGE

Asking For Help is a Superpower, too!

When you have a growth mindset, you know that asking for help is a superpower. Sometimes, when we are thinking with a fixed mindset, we may think that asking for help makes us weak. That's not true!

Everyone who does great things has had help!
Michael Jordan had a team of other basketball players who could help him.

Our favorite poet, Amanda Gorman, had other poets to talk to whenever she felt nervous.
Yay for help!

Your mission today is to ask for help 5 times.
(Any kind of help is okay.) Also, remember to say, "Thank you" when someone helps you.

Every time you ask for help, color one section on the number 5 until the entire number has been colored. You've got this!

Today's Challenge: Ask for help 5 times.

This is your **"Help Me"** Tracker!

Color one section on the number 5 until the
entire number has been colored.
You've got this!

"ASKING for HELP IS A SUPERPOWER"

You Matter

CONNECTION TIME

When we have a growth mindset, we know that people can learn, grow, and change. This means that sometimes people can have new ideas or think differently than before.

But, sometimes, we don't take time to get to know people we care about again and again and again. Instead, we think we already know them.

That's why it's great to have connection time and get to know people we love again and let them get to know us again.

CHOOSE SOMEONE TO BE YOUR CONNECTION BUDDY

My Connection Buddy's name
(Your Connection Buddy can also be your Challenge Friend.)

INTERVIEW TIME

DAY 4

Take turns asking and answering questions with your buddy. Listen carefully to one another.

ME

MY BUDDY

1. If you could have any superpower, what would it be? Why?

2. What is something you wish we did more together?

3. Why are you proud of me?

3. What makes you feel safe? Have you ever felt unsafe before?

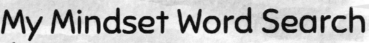

My Mindset Word Search

Day 4

Can you find the words below?
Circle each word in the word search!

PRAISE   BRAVE   FIXED
TRY   MINDSET GROWTH

```
M  K  P  R  A  I  S  E
F  I  X  E  D  B  G  C
R  D  N  W  X  R  L  N
I  M  V  D  O  A  O  A
E  P  B  W  S  V  V  D
N  T  T  R  Y  E  E  L
D  H  S  I  N  G  T  B
```

My Reminder for Hard Days

Use this for your hard days! Write Growth Mindset messages in the bubbles to make you smile on days that challenge you! Then, write yourself a secret message below!

The more I try, the more my brain grows!

Draw Your Picture

I can't wait to help other people when I get better at this!

I am a ROCKSTAR!

Write a Secret Message for yourself to read on a hard day!

DAY 4 CHALLENGE

You are making a difference!

Sometimes, the best way to learn something really well is to teach it to someone else. What's also beautiful about teaching something to another person is that you can make a difference in their life by showing them something new.
When you teach others, you help them grow.

Your final mission is to find one person and teach them all about what it means to have a growth mindset and what it means to have a fixed mindset.

You can use the next page to draw or write what you need for your lesson.

Thank you for making a difference!

Today's Challenge: Teach one person how to have a growth mindset.

You Can Do Hard Things

DAY 5

SOMEONE YOU ADMIRE

Think of someone you think is amazing.
It can be someone you don't know in real life.
Who are they? Why are they amazing?

_____

_____

_____

Draw something they do well.

Now, think of three positive words to describe that person. Write each word in a circle.

On the lines below, think of ways that those positive words may also describe you.

I am also _____ because I

_____

I am also _____ because I

_____

I am also _____ because I

_____

Oftentimes, we have the same positive qualities that we see in others, but it can be harder to see them in ourselves. You are special!

DAY 5 CHALLENGE

You can do hard things.

You have people who love and support you.
You can encourage yourself even when others don't know what to say. You can do hard things!

When things are "hard," they are often challenging us to grow. People who have a growth mindset regularly do challenging things to help grow their brains.

For example, some people who have a growth mindset practice brushing their teeth with the opposite hand that they usually brush their teeth with.
This is a challenge that can help their brains grow.

Some people learn something new.

Your challenge today is to look at the "something new" list and grow your brain by memorizing or learning something that you didn't know before.

You can do hard things!

Final Challenge:
Learn something new.

SOMETHING NEW LIST

Grow your brain by choosing one new skill to learn from the list. You can also choose a skill that is not on the list. Learn something new!
Then, show your new skill to someone you love.

1. Learn to count to 10 in Spanish.
2. Learn to count to 10 in French.
3. Learn to sign the numbers 1 to 10 using American Sign Language.
1. Learn to count to 10 in Mandarin.
2. Learn to count to 10 in Korean.
3. Memorize the names and order of the planets.
4. Learn to skip count to 100 by 10s.
5. Learn to skip count to 100 by 5s.
6. Memorize "Don't Quit" by John Greenleaf Whittier.
7. Learn how to spell your name. (Try American Sign Language.)
8. Memorize the colors of the rainbow. (ROYGBIV)

I chose to

_____

_____

I showed my new skill to (Who)

_____

Not Yet, But I Will TRY!

Think of something that you are not very good at...YET!
Practice makes perfect! Think of ways that you can get better!
You can do it!

Day 5

But, if I...

Start Here:
I'm not good at ...

Yet!

HELLO! This Is Me!

And if I...

Then, I will...

I will get better!

My TRY Ladder

Welcome to your TRY Ladder!
Write a goal that you want to meet at the top of the ladder.
Then, write what you can do to accomplish your goal!

Day 5

Finally, I will . . .

Then, I will . . .

My Big GOAL is to:

Then, I will . . .

I will do a dance every time i climb the ladder!

Tomorrow, I will . . .

I am a ROCKSTAR!

Today, I can . . .

My TRY Ladder

Welcome to your TRY Ladder!
Write a goal that you want to meet at the top of the ladder.
Then, write what you can do to accomplish your goal!

Finally, I will...
give my whole presentation to my friends

Then, I will...
practice in front of the mirror daily

Then, I will...
Ask my teacher for feedback and help.

Tomorrow, I will...
Start writing a script for my presentation

Today, I can...
plan out what I want to talk about.

My Big GOAL is to:
Give an amazing presentation

I will do a dance every time i climb the ladder!

I am a ROCKSTAR!

CERTIFICATE
OF
PARTICIPATION

This is granted to

_____

for completing the ten-day
Growth Mindset Challenge

_____

Your Challenge Friend

Gahmya Teacher

Gahmya Drummond-Bey

Evolved Teacher, Inc

CPSIA information can be obtained
at www.ICGtesting.com
Printed in the USA
BVHW022316010322
630318BV00002B/15